"*The Jericho Fast* is a biblical and practical way to grow in spiritual understanding, wisdom, and transformational revelation. When applied, the revelation in this book will shift your life to a place of breakthrough. Rhoda is a phenomenal leader, minister, and intercessor. She has been through the fire in her own life, and she knows what it means to walk in obedience with a lifestyle of prayer and fasting. After you have done all, stand and see God grant great victories. I highly recommend *The Jericho Fast*! It will greatly bless your life!"

—RACHEL JOY KNIGHT, Pastor and Co-Founder of Story Life Church in Apopka, Florida

"One of the best books I've read in a long time. Anointed and powerful, yet simple. The book outlines a plan for spiritual warfare with power-packed scriptures and prayers. She talks you through the whole fast. I absolutely enjoyed it!"

—PASTOR THOMAS HICKS, Founder of Christian Assemblies Ministry in Stewartsville, New Jersey

"We have been doing fasting for years. We believe this book is an easy to use guide for those who are new to fasting, but also an asset for seasoned believers and anyone looking to draw closer to the Lord. Each chapter is filled with scripture along with helpful and meaningful explanations. We also really loved the prayers at the end of each chapter. 'The Last Lap' chapter especially touched our hearts. We are sure it will touch many more, inspiring them to press on and finish the race."

—ERNEST AND JOAN STANLEY, Pastors of Shepherd's House Christian Outreach in Severn, Maryland

"*The Jericho Fast* truly inspired me. As soon as I began reading in 'Day One' about God giving Joshua instructions, I knew the Lord was leading me to start the fast. Having just completed the fast, I can truly sense that walls were knocked down in my life. I'm excited to see what the Lord has in store!"

—BECKY WHARTON, Youth Pastor of Ministries for Christ in Newark, Delaware

"This book is a dynamic teaching on the underutilized yet powerful tools of prayer and fasting. In our day, time is of the essence, and success is the only option! This book is biblically sound and easy read. It will help you understand how to integrate fasting as a practical tool."

—DAWN WORKMAN, Founder of Where Pearls Prosper

THE JERICHO FAST

How to Break through Walls with Prayer and Fasting

Rhoda Faye Diehl

CALLED WRITERS

CHRISTIAN PUBLISHING

Published by Called Writers Christian Publishing, LLC

Tuscaloosa, Alabama

ISBN 978-1-7354760-0-1

CONTENTS

Introduction: A Hard Place   9

The Jericho Prayer   11
What to Know Before You Fast   13
Reasons to Fast   17
Choosing Your Fast   19
Day One   29
Getting Started
Day Two   35
Look Up
Day Three   39
Personal Revelation
Day Four   49
Scouting the Land
Moments of Weakness   57
Day Five   61
Keep Silent
Day Six   67
Walking Around the Walls
Day Seven   75
Victory
Keep Walking in Victory   83

Meet Called Writers   87
Recent Releases from Called Writers   89
About the Author   91

INTRODUCTION: A HARD PLACE

From time to time, in life, we find ourselves stuck. We've come upon a hard place—a place that has us trapped. We can't seem to move forward. There is an area of our life that just won't change, no matter how hard we try or how much we pray.

Get ready for the walls to come down.

This book is your answer. We're going to learn some kingdom keys on prayer and fasting. We're going to change the way we think. We will learn how to walk in authority. We will gain strength and courage to move forward.

Just like the Israelites marched around the walls of Jericho for 7 days, we're going to march around the walls in our life—the ones that won't move. We will march around them with 7 days of prayer and fasting, and they will fall in Jesus' name.

The Lord Himself will knock down the walls in front of you. The enemy has tried his best to block you. He wants to keep you out of your promised land. He even tries to use these walls as weapons against you. He tells you lies. That you'll never get free. That it's over. There's no point in trying. That the situation is hopeless.

No more!

The Lord is saying, "Through your prayers and your faith, I'm tearing these walls down! No more will the enemy hinder your blessings or stop you from seeing what's on the other side of this pain. It's time to charge through the rubble and leave all the troubles behind!"

It's time to take the city.

It's time to take authority.

Somebody ought to shout:

The walls are coming down!

THE JERICHO PRAYER

Heavenly Father, just as You used Joshua to lead the Israelites, Lord, let the Holy Spirit lead us in this time of prayer and fasting.

Give us the instructions for our victory just like You did for Joshua. Equip us, Lord, with power and strength.

Give us the courage to overcome what is standing in front of us. Lead the way.

We know it's not by our power, but by You and through You, that we will destroy the walls in our life.

Lord, we are standing on Your promises. We believe and trust in You. In Jesus' name, amen.

WHAT TO KNOW BEFORE YOU FAST

W hen we fast, we are acknowledging that we need spiritual help. We are humbling ourselves and acknowledging that we cannot solve our own problem. We're acknowledging that the natural isn't enough, and that we need to tap into the spiritual.

We're exercising our faith in God by saying, "Lord, I cannot fix this on my own. I can't bring down these walls. Nothing good is going to happen unless You move!"

The Bible, as well as Christian history, has much to tell us about prayer and fasting. There are just a few quick things I'd like to note here.

Fasting is a Personal Event

When you fast, do not look somber as the hypocrites do, for they disfigure their faces to show men they are fasting. I tell you the truth, they have received their reward in full. But when you fast, put oil on your head and wash your face, so that it will not be obvious to men that you are fasting, but only to your Father, who is unseen; and your Father, who sees what is done in secret will reward you. – Matthew 6:16-18 (NIV)

You Can Fast from Things Besides Food

The husband should fulfill his marital duty to his wife, and likewise the wife to her husband. The wife does not have authority over her own body but yields it to her husband. In the same way, the husband does not have authority over his own body but yields it to his wife. Do not deprive each other except perhaps by mutual consent and for a time, so that you may devote yourselves to prayer. Then come together again so that Satan will not tempt you because of your lack of self-control. – 1 Corinthians 7:3-5 (NIV)

Jesus Noted That His Followers Would Fast

They said to him, "John's disciples often fast and pray, and so do the disciples of the Pharisees, but yours go on eating and drinking." Jesus answered, "Can you make the friends of the bridegroom fast while he is with them? But the time will come when the bridegroom will be taken from them; in those days they will fast. – Luke 5:33-35 (NIV)

Fasting is a Form of Worship

And there was a prophetess, Anna, the daughter of Phanuel, of the tribe of Asher. She was advanced in years, having lived with her husband seven years from when she was a virgin, and then as a widow until she was eighty-four. She did not depart from the temple, worshiping with fasting and prayer night and day. – Luke 2:36–37 (ESV)

Fasting is Powerful

Moses, Elijah, Ezekiel, and Daniel fasted and prayed. Jesus fasted for forty days. Paul and the early Christians fasted. The early church fasted on Wednesdays and Fridays. Martin Luther was criticized for fasting "too much." John Calvin fasted and prayed until the greater part of Geneva turned to God. John Knox fasted and prayed, and the wicked Queen Mary of Scotland (aka Bloody Mary) said she feared no armed force as much as she feared the prayers of John Knox.

Jonathan Edwards, who was God's instrument in a revival known as the Great Awakening, fasted and prayed. He was not known to be an eloquent or powerful speaker, but God would move to save thousands when he preached. He credited this to prayer and fasting.

John Wesley, who also saw thousands respond when he preached, fasted twice a week. Charles Finney, one of the greatest spiritual leaders in history, was a man who fasted and prayed. Evangelist D. L. Moody was another great Christian leader who often fasted and prayed.

REASONS TO FAST

There are various reasons to fast and each person's circumstances will be different. However, the Bible does give us plenty of examples. The biblical accounts often include a specific reason the person or group fasted. Here are a few such examples.

Praying for Health or a Crisis Situation

David pleaded with God for the child. He fasted and went into his house and spent the nights lying on the ground. – 2 Samuel 12:16 (BSB)

Praying for Safety and Protection

There, by the Ahava Canal, I proclaimed a fast, so that we might humble ourselves before our God and ask him for a safe journey for us and our children, with all our possessions. – Ezra 8:21 (NIV).

As an Act of Repentance

When they had assembled at Mizpah, they drew water and poured it out before the LORD. On that day they fasted and there they confessed, "We have sinned against the LORD." – 1 Samuel 7:6 (NIV)

As a Sign of Mourning

They mourned and wept and fasted till evening for Saul and his son Jonathan, and for the army of the LORD and the nation of Israel, because they had fallen by the sword. – 2 Samuel 1:12 (NIV)

Before Starting Ministry

Paul and Barnabas appointed elders for them in each church and, with prayer and fasting, committed them to the Lord, in whom they had put their trust. – Acts 14:23 (NIV)

Praying for Victory

Alarmed, Jehoshaphat resolved to inquire of the Lord, and he proclaimed a fast for all Judah. The people of Judah came together to seek help from the Lord; indeed, they came from every town in Judah to seek him. – 2 Chronicles 20:3-4 (NIV)

CHOOSING YOUR FAST

There are four main types of fasts we can consider. Each one has different aspects, so the choice of fast will largely depend on the circumstances and goals of each individual.

Total Fast

In this type of fast, no food is eaten. There are several examples in the Bible of extended total fasts. Both Jesus and Moses fasted for 40 days, but those examples are miraculous. Outside of the miraculous, total fasts should be limited to three days for most people. Though some people with more experience do choose to fast longer.

Selective Fast

Some people only choose to give up certain foods. There is an example of this in Daniel chapter 10. Daniel says that for three weeks, he ate no "delicacies" or "choice foods." He also did not eat meat or drink wine during that time. You could give up certain foods, do only a liquid diet (e.g. smoothies, juices), etc. The point is to deny the flesh and devote yourself to prayer, so you can choose to give up some of the things that you know your flesh really wants. Just be sure to think through any medical implications, and consult physicians when appropriate. Use wisdom.

Time of Day Fast

Sometimes people choose, during an extended period of time, not to eat during certain hours of the day. For example, the Jews sometimes used to fast during daylight hours on certain days and at certain times of the year.

Soul Fast

Sometimes people give up things like TV, music, or social media when they fast. This is especially helpful when people have medical problems that prevent them from doing food-related fasts. 1 Corinthians 7:5 describes a married couple mutually agreeing to fast from sexual relations so that they can devote themselves to prayer.

What Not to Do

There are a few things we should not do in regard to fasting. First, we should never fast to impress others. Also, we shouldn't allow our fasting to become an undue burden on others. We should consult our spouse and children beforehand and make sure they are willing to walk through this with us. They don't have to fast with us, but they should understand that it will affect our home environment and our relationships. We'll be drawing near to God and away from normal activities.

God set up times of feasting and times of fasting in the Bible. He likes and blesses both of these things, so He doesn't generally want us to miss times of feasting and celebration with our families and communities. The point is, we shouldn't think we have to make fasting any harder than it already is by choosing to fast during holidays or other such events. There will always be some challenges to fasting, but as an example, we shouldn't take it on ourselves to fast Thanksgiving or Christmas.

After praying and thinking about it, pick one of the types of fasts to do for the next 7 days. Choose wisely. The more fleshly desires you give up, the more of God's presence and power that can be released into your life.

But you also want to make a commitment that you know you can hold to.

In the story of Joshua, in chapter 2, we see that he first scouted out the land. Joshua didn't just charge into the city. He wasn't anxious. He employed wisdom by sending in spies first. He wanted to make sure the walls of Jericho were going to fall. But that result wouldn't come by being hasty, rash, or foolish. When we fast, we have to think through the kind of commitment we're making. We don't want to set ourselves up for failure, but we do want to make a significant commitment.

One thing to keep in mind is that if you start out with a selective fast, you can always take it up a notch later on. So for example, you could start out on day one just fasting meat, bread, and sweets. By day three, as you're getting closer to God and denying your flesh, you might decide to do liquids only. By day five, you might decide to do the last three days in a total fast.

What you don't want to do, especially if you have never fasted, is start out overly zealous, decide hastily that you're going to do a 7 day total fast, and then end up eating on day two.

Ask for Wisdom

So, step one, pray before you fast and ask the Holy Spirit to give you wisdom and guidance:

Dear Heavenly Father, I come to You, Lord, with a humble heart and ask You to strengthen me for this battle. Show me what I need to fast, and reveal to me what I need to do before I undertake this time of fasting and prayer. Give me the wisdom and strength to overcome fear of this situation. Go before me and put a hedge of protection over me. Cover me in the blood, in Jesus' name, Amen.

When you humble yourself in this way, the Lord will give you spiritual eyes and a spiritual outlook. Then you can be aware and alert and awake, like Rahab. She was spared from destruction because she helped hide the spies who had come there from Israel. It was because of her willing spirit *and her faithfulness* that she was spared. Not only did she make a deal to hide the spies, she followed through. She did her part.

This is just my best guess, but I believe Rahab was already praying to the God of Israel to spare her and her family from the impending judgment on Jericho. When the two spies came through, she believed it was the providential opportunity for which she had been praying, and she began to demonstrate her faith by action.

This is your opportunity. You've been asking for a way out of your situation. You've been stuck for a long time. You've asked for change, but it hasn't come yet. God is giving you a way out. He's offering to rescue you and your family, but you have to make a commitment and then be faithful.

You're going to do it.

You're not going to fail this time.

God is going to see you through!

How God Gave Me This Revelation

Around 20 years or so ago, I didn't know a thing about prayer and fasting. I was clueless. Growing up in a Christian home and going to Christian schools, I learned how to pray in a casual way, but that was about it.

Like most of us, I experienced a lot of hurt and rejection growing up. But I didn't really understand why my life was such a mess. I would sit and have pity parties for myself, and that eventually led to depression. Eventually, that depression became oppression. I looked for answers everywhere but God.

So I made bad decision after bad decision. Those led me to all kinds of dead ends. By the age of 25, I was twice divorced. I also had two kids with two different fathers.

The devil had me thinking this was it—no one was ever going to love me or want me. I started getting very down on myself, and I even started hating my own appearance. The devil had my mind so twisted.

Time went on and these problems, these issues, these mental and emotional strongholds, just kept building.

It was like the devil was building a wall in front of me, brick by brick, to trap me. I couldn't move forward. All I knew how to do was keep living the way I was living. I had gotten used to my lifestyle and eventually just accepted that this was the way things were going to be.

In 2008, my mother got really sick with breast cancer. Prior to that, she had already stood firm in faith and beat the cancer for 10 years. But when it came back, it was very aggressive. The cancer spread into her lungs and even her bones. But she was the true definition of a woman of faith. She never gave up on being healed. She would fast and pray like nobody's business.

She never once complained or got upset with God.

Every morning, she would take her medicine and read her Bible verses. She would say them out loud as she took the medicine. I'd say, "Mom, why do you do that?"

She would respond, "I'm digesting His Word. It's my spiritual medicine."

Back then, I still didn't fully understand the power of prayer. I also was completely unaware that God was working through my mother's example to teach me some kingdom keys about prayer.

Right before my mother passed away, she talked to me about those kingdom keys. She told me to always put God first, never stop praying, and be a godly mother to my kids.

Now those three things put together may sound like a simple and obvious strategy, but the real key is in executing the plan. Marching around walls for 7 days and then blowing horns at the end—that's a simple plan. But the Israelites had to go out and execute it. In other words, they had to actually go out and get the job done.

Somehow I started getting these things done after my mother passed on to Heaven. I learned to fast and pray. I would ask God to help me and bless my life, and He began to answer. Jesus came to my rescue, and walls began to fall down all around me.

Walls of hate.

Regret.

Confusion.

Depression.

Generational curses.

Hurt.

Rejection.

They all came crashing down.

Once those walls came down, it opened doors for God to be able to bless me in other ways. God sent me my Boaz—my knight in shining armor. We married, and I thank God for my husband every day. My entire life has been changed from the inside out.

Even though He had already done more than I ever dreamed, God wasn't finished. All of a sudden my entire life was like Joseph's moment of going from the pit to the palace. God did some "suddenlies" for me and my family. He even gave me spiritual gifts, and after that He gave me a thriving ministry.

The Jericho fast is a very powerful tool that we can use to go out and execute God's battle plan for our lives.

He wants to knock down the walls.

He's ready.

He's waiting on you.

Let's go!

Prayer

Lord, there's a wall that's tall, but I know my call. I must have faith like Joshua.

No time to sit.

These days and times, I must rise to the call. I must pray more and apply Your Word more than ever. I must be courageous and have no fear except fear of the Lord.

The battle has already been won.

Lord, I know it's up to me. It's up to me to proceed to victory.

I've stayed here long enough. It's time to get tough. It's time to go into battle. I have tried everything that this world could offer, but got no results. Lord, I'm ready to rise to the call.

For the LORD your God is the one who goes with you to fight for you against your enemies to give you victory. – Deuteronomy 20:4 (NIV)

DAY ONE
GETTING STARTED

Okay, so you're feeling inspired. You've got your battle plan. You're ready to go out in formation. You're ready to march. You're ready to fight for your family. Your future. Your life.

That's all good, but when you march out, those walls are still standing there. They're surrounding you. So far, you've just been wandering around inside these walls. Looking up at them, wondering how they're ever going to move.

The longer you stay, the bigger the wall gets. Every day new bricks get added by the enemy. Those bricks have names, and we're going to call them out right now.

Doubt.

Fear.

Negative thinking.

Generational curses.

Suicide.

Hate.

Anger.

Unforgiveness.

Depression.

Oppression.

Addictions.

Sickness.

Disease.

Violence.

Rage.

Malice.

Covetousness.

Self-righteousness.

Pride.

Dishonesty.

Discontentment.

Let's call these out for what they are—lies! When these feel like walls in our lives that we cannot escape from, they are lies. Yes, sin enslaves. The enemy enslaves.

That enslavement is real, but it's based on a lie. The truth is this: Christ came to give us freedom, and who the Son sets free is free indeed!

The number one thing the enemy loves to do is remind us of our past. He would always be whispering in my ear things like, "You're not good enough."

"Nobody wants you."

"Nobody likes you."

"You're never going to amount to anything."

Boy, it would work too. It was a constant struggle back then.

But when I was feeling beat up and in need of encouragement, the Lord would always remind me of the story of the Walls of Jericho.

This story empowers us to be strong and of good courage. Yes, Joshua is a book that is very old. It's full of literal battles and wars, but the Book of Joshua is extremely relevant for Christians today.

We are living in days of battle and spiritual struggle. We need to know how to fight. We need to know that our God is able to give victory.

We need to know how to follow Him to that victory.

Joshua teaches us how to do all of these things!

Joshua 6

Now the gates of Jericho were securely barred because of the Israelites. No one went out and no one came in.

Then the Lord said to Joshua, "See, I have delivered Jericho into your hands, along with its king and its fighting men. March around the city once with all the armed men. Do this for six days. Have seven priests carry trumpets of rams' horns in front of the ark. On the seventh day, march around the city seven times, with the priests blowing the trumpets. When you hear them sound a long blast on the trumpets, have the whole army give a loud shout; then the wall of the city will collapse and the army will go up, everyone straight in." – Joshua 6:1-5 (NIV)

The Lord gave Joshua some instructions. The end result was going to be that the walls would fall so the Israelites could go in and take the city.

How many times has the Lord given us instructions and we fail to follow them?

Joshua could have done that. He could have said, "This plan seems crazy. There's no way it will work. I think we'll just get some battering rams instead."

Imagine what the outcome would have been for him and his people.

A lot of times the reason we fail is that we try to fix our own problems. We try to take matters into our own hands instead of following God's very simple instructions.

When we do that, we interfere with God's plan.

The plan that God gave to us gets derailed, and of course, the enemy comes in to take advantage of the situation. Not only did we not get our answer, we just let the enemy add more bricks to our wall.

So how did Joshua avoid doing what we often do? How did he make it through all the temptations to doubt, fear, give up, or go his own way? How did he get to the point of seeing victory?

Keep going.

Keep fasting.

Keep praying.

As we'll see in tomorrow's chapter, Joshua first humbled himself. That's what you're doing right now.

Prayer

Lord, I humble myself today. I acknowledge that I cannot fix my own problem. Without You, I cannot heal. I cannot bless. I cannot restore. Those things only come through You.

There is no answer for me in the natural. Thank You for the chance to put off the natural and access Your supernatural power and presence.

Thank You, Lord, for this wonderful opportunity—this amazing tool called fasting that You've given to us. Please strengthen me and help me to be obedient. Help me to complete this task.

In Jesus' name I pray, amen.

DAY TWO
LOOK UP

Now when Joshua was near Jericho, he looked up and saw a man standing in front of him with a drawn sword in his hand. Joshua went up to him and asked, "Are you for us or for our enemies?"

"Neither," he replied, "but as commander of the army of the Lord I have now come." **Then Joshua fell facedown to the ground in reverence, and asked him, "What message does my Lord have for his servant?"** – Joshua 5:13-14 (NIV)

Why did Joshua ask an angel whose side he was on?

Better yet, why did the angel say he was on neither side?

I bet Joshua felt like that was a smack in his face. He probably thought the angel was there to fix his problem for him.

Instead, the angel seems to have had a bit of an attitude with Joshua. It's almost like he was saying, "Forget whose side I'm on—whose side are you on, Joshua?"

That can apply to us today. Are you on the world's side?

You know you're supposed to be on the Lord's side, but are you really?

Do you still have one foot in the world?

Do you still have a few irons in the world's fire?

How serious are you?

Are you ready to take this to the next level?

Yes?

Okay.

"And Joshua fell on his face to the earth and worshiped." (v. 14 ESV)

When Joshua fell on his face and worshiped, he recognized who was standing in front of him. The Lord had Joshua right where He wanted him—on his knees, praying and worshiping.

When we fall on our knees and bow our hearts to the King of Kings, we are recognizing His authority and ushering in His presence. At His feet—that's right where we belong.

When Joshua looked up, what did he see? Was he looking at the wall standing in front of him? Was he focused on the obstacles?

No!

He was looking at the angel of the Lord. The Lord had sent His angel to let Joshua see something besides the walls. God wanted Joshua's eyes on Him.

A lot of times when we're faced with a situation that hasn't moved for a very long time, it's all we can see. There's a giant wall, and our nose is all the way up against it. When we stare too long at this wall, we lose our focus on God. Discouragement starts to settle in. Then along comes good 'ol doubt. Fear always seems to tag along too. They're buddies.

God wants us to take a step back.

Your Jericho has you trapped, mentally and emotionally. You've been looking at it way too long. You can't get away from it. Even when you forget about it for a little while, it comes back to your mind. It creeps in, even during the good moments.

It's always with you. You can't seem to get away from it. You think about it day in and day out. It gets your attention. It's in your face.

That's why this part of the story is so vital. We tend to jump right past this part and pay more attention to the end. But when we try to skip parts of it, we'll never make it to the end.

This is the beginning of Joshua taking instructions from the Lord. He first had to fix his eyes on the commander of the Lord's army. All of Joshua's attention is now on the Lord. He's not even looking at the wall. Like Joshua, we must have our eyes fixed on the Lord before we'll be ready to do what He says.

Prayer

Lord, fix my eyes on Jesus. Help me to step back away from this wall and see You clearly. My problems seem so big, but You are so much bigger, Lord! Let my eyes see You clearly today—the author and perfecter of my faith. In Jesus' name, amen.

DAY THREE
PERSONAL REVELATION

Before Joshua can go any further, he has to get a revelation—a personal notice that the Lord is speaking to him. The Lord is going to tell Joshua what to do in order to bring these walls down. But before He gives Joshua the instructions, He first has to make sure Joshua is paying full attention.

Joshua was a leader. He had to lead others down this path.

Are you a leader in your home? Your church? Your office? Notice I didn't say "the" leader. I said, "a leader." We're all leaders at some level or in some capacity.

You may have to help others along the way. There may be other people who are going to walk this path of freedom and blessing with you.

It required great faith from Joshua because not only did he have to lead himself to be obedient, he had to lead others to do the same. The elders and the nation needed faith too. It took great faith to follow Joshua in this plan. Faith comes by hearing, and hearing by the Word of God. So let's take a few minutes to soak up some of God's Word. Read this passage out loud.

I lift up my eyes to the hills.

From where does my help come?

My help comes from the Lord,

who made heaven and earth.

He will not let your foot be moved;

he who keeps you will not slumber.

Behold, he who keeps Israel

will neither slumber nor sleep.

The Lord is your keeper;

the Lord is your shade on your right hand.

The sun shall not strike you by day,

nor the moon by night.

The Lord will keep you from all evil;

he will keep your life.

The Lord will keep your going out and your

coming in from this time forth and forevermore. – Psalm 121:1-8 (ESV)

Read it out loud one more time. This time, say it like you mean it!

Holy Ground

And the commander of the Lord's army said to Joshua, "Take off your sandals from your feet, for the place where you are standing is holy." And Joshua did so. – Joshua 5:15 (ESV)

The first instruction the commander of the Lord's army gave to Joshua is kind of strange: "Take off your sandals, for the place where you are standing is holy."

Why did the angel tell him to take off his sandals? There are several different things sandals, or shoes, can represent here. We'll go through each one.

Our Past

The sandals were from his past. His sandals represented the wilderness, they carried the dust and the muck that he'd picked up all those years out in the desert. How do I know that? The Bible says they had worn the same shoes for 40 years.

Yet the LORD says, "During the forty years that I led you through the wilderness, your clothes did not wear out, nor did the sandals on your feet." – Deuteronomy 29:5 (ESV)

God wanted him to walk clean on the new ground. This ground was Holy—set apart unto the Lord. So Joshua obeyed.

When God wants to do a new thing in your life, there are some requirements. No one pours new wine into old wineskins. When the Lord is about to take you into your promised land, you can't bring the old. You have to get rid of anything that would hinder you. Is the Lord bringing anything to your mind right now? Maybe take a minute and ask the Lord: "Lord, is there anything in my home, my life, or my heart that needs to go?"

If so, throw it in the garbage. Delete it off of your computer or your DVR. Call that person and tell them you forgive them. Call that other person and tell them you're sorry, and ask them to forgive you. If it's a hurt and that person is long gone from your life or no longer alive, then just lay it at the Lord's feet and ask Him to take it.

If nothing is coming to mind right now, that's okay. There will be plenty of time for that. The Lord will show you things as you go. And where you're going, there's going to be some sacrificing of the flesh. So we're laying down our appetites.

That's what fasting is—denying our flesh so that the spirit can grow stronger. But fasting *isn't just denying the flesh*. We also have to stay in prayer. If we're not praying, we're just on a diet.

And don't think for one second the enemy won't try to trip you up and distract you. That's why the Lord sent his angel to instruct Joshua. Joshua needed to take some precautions and prepare. He needed to take the right attitude and posture and get his mind right, so he wouldn't get sidetracked.

Readiness

In the Bible, and generally in ancient times, shoes represented readiness. While listing and explaining the armor of God, Paul mentions and explains shoes:

"and, as shoes for your feet, having put on the readiness given by the gospel of peace." – Ephesians 6:15 (ESV)

To a man about to lead an army into battle, shoes probably represented his ability to go out and get the job done. When you take off your shoes, you're acknowledging that you're about to be still. You're not headed out to take care of business on your own.

Victory

Shoes can also represent victory over the enemy. One thing we see in Old Testament times is that the leaders of a victorious army would go and place their feet on the neck of the enemy.

When they had brought these kings to Joshua, he summoned all the men of Israel and said to the army commanders who had come with him, "Come here and put your feet on the necks of these kings." So they came forward and placed their feet on their necks. – Joshua 10:24 (NIV)

Tying It All Together

In order to have the Lord fighting for Him, Joshua needed to lay down things from his past. He also needed to recognize that he couldn't move forward on his own. He was in the presence of Holy greatness. It was time for him to acknowledge that this was something he could not do through his own efforts.

He could not lead these people into the promised land by himself. He could not conquer these lands alone. He could not bring down the walls of Jericho. He had to put his trust in the Lord. Joshua had to acknowledge that God alone had the power to accomplish this great work. In the same way, we must humble ourselves before Him and worship His holy name. Then we can move forward into His victory.

When Joshua obeyed the command to take off his shoes, he put his trust in the Lord. Let's take a moment to humble ourselves before the Lord, and worship Him.

Let's take off our shoes, and acknowledge that we're now on Holy ground.

How to Be Strong, Courageous, and Successful

Be strong and courageous, because you will lead these people to inherit the land I swore to their ancestors to give them. "Be strong and very courageous. Be careful to obey all the law my servant Moses gave you; do not turn from it to the right or to the left, that you may be successful wherever you go. Keep this Book of the Law always on your lips; meditate on it day and night, so that you may be careful to do everything written in it. Then you will be prosperous and successful. Have I not commanded you? Be strong and courageous. Do not be afraid; do not be discouraged, for the LORD your God will be with you wherever you go." – Joshua 1:6-9 (NIV)

The Lord told Joshua three times to be strong and courageous. Why? The purpose of these commands is to help Joshua take his eyes off of himself, his challenges, his weaknesses, and his enemies. Instead he had to fix his eyes on the source of true strength and courage. The Lord was encouraging Joshua to be prayed up for what was ahead.

It's like the Lord was saying, "Joshua, it may look big, but don't let that put fear into you. Don't let the size of those walls discourage you. Joshua, you've got this."

The Lord tells him to meditate on His words day and night. God invented meditation way before the false religions came up with their counterfeits. God telling Joshua to wake up with the Word. Go to bed with the Word. Because if you can meditate on God's Word, then it goes from your brain to your heart.

Joshua was probably walking around repeating these words to himself over and over out loud, "Be strong and courageous. Do not be afraid."

Joshua had to lock that word in so that he could defeat the enemy. He knew there were big obstacles, but the Lord was preparing him to move forward without fear.

Right now, you need to be encouraged and have the kind of faithfulness Joshua had. Don't be discouraged or dismayed. Don't lose hope. Instead, meditate on the Word of God. Let it get deep within your heart. Read these passages over and over, out loud.

When it gets into you, deep within your heart, this empowers you to overcome fear. Trust the Lord. Listen to His instructions. He's taking you to a place where you'll have to remove anything that would interfere with His presence.

Don't let anything hold you back from walking into your divine destiny. Your miracle. Your breakthrough. Your deliverance. Call it *yours*!

This is where your victory begins.

Say, "Lord, I'm willing. Here I am, ready to stand on Holy ground."

Empty Ourselves

In order for our walls to come down, we have to empty ourselves. We must allow the Holy Spirit to dwell in us and fill us up. Our body is the temple of the Lord, and we must keep it spotless—ready for the Lord's coming. The Holy Spirit won't dwell anywhere that is unclean.

When we fast, we're removing anything that might interfere with God's presence. The Bible gives us examples of people who fasted and prayed, using different types of fasts for different reasons. All of them produced positive results.

Remember, many of the Old Testament heroes of the faith fasted and prayed. The followers of John the Baptist fasted and prayed. Jesus fasted and prayed. Jesus' disciples fasted and prayed. Many in the early church fasted and prayed.

We ought to fast and pray.

Fasting is intentionally denying the flesh in order to gain a response from the spirit. It means renouncing the natural in order to invoke the supernatural.

To fast requires more than what we might initially think. Fasting is really restricting yourself of self— putting off self and instead renewing our minds with the Word of God, just like Joshua.

Now we've got our shoes off. We're humbling ourselves. We're acknowledging that it can't be accomplished by the natural. We're fasting. We're praying. We're renewing our minds with God's Word.

Tomorrow, it will be time to go and scout out our surroundings.

Prayer

Lord, thank You for giving me personal revelation. Thank You for showing me the things, people, and places I need to set down or turn away from. Thank You for helping me to acknowledge that I cannot do any of this without You.

I humble myself before You. You alone are powerful. You alone are good. You alone are worthy of praise.

Please help me to meditate on Your Word today and every day, so that I can be strong, courageous, prosperous, and successful. Please help me to empty my mind and heart of sin and self, and to fill it with Your Word, Your truth, Your goodness, Your light, and Your love.

I am Your servant. I surrender myself to You, to do with me according to Your good pleasure, in Jesus' name, amen.

DAY FOUR

SCOUTING THE LAND

After the Lord gave Joshua some initial instructions to help him humble himself and get focused, Joshua's next step was to go evaluate the problem. The two scouts (or spies) were Joshua's eyes.

The scouts went into the promised land and Rahab looked after them. They both brought back a good report to Joshua:

"The LORD has surely given the whole land into our hands; all the people are melting in fear because of us." – Joshua 2:24 (ISV)

Another purpose the Lord had planned for these two scouts was to save Rahab and her family. The spies are not named. This is different from the 12 spies Moses had sent into the promised land 40 years prior. They are all listed by name and tribe in Numbers chapter one.

Sometimes we are doing God's work out in the open, and other times we are doing it with no recognition from people. Even if no one knows who we are or what we're doing, God sees what's happening. Our labor is making a difference, and we're storing up treasures in eternity.

The actions of these two spies affected the family tree of Jesus as well, since Rahab appears in his bloodline. She became the mother of Boaz, who was the kinsman-redeemer of Ruth. Ruth had a son named Obed, who was the grandfather of King David. Of course, Jesus was a descendant of David's bloodline.

We never know how our actions might affect others. The fast you're on right now could affect future generations for years to come. It could have a significant effect on the world!

Joshua couldn't have had any idea how his actions affected future generations and the world. We can't see that far ahead either, but we know that our actions are important. God didn't arrange all of this and have us fasting if He didn't have a significant reason for doing it.

With that said, let's look at the story from Joshua Chapter 2 and see what else we can glean from it.

After this, Nun's son Joshua sent two men from the Acacia groves as undercover scouts. He told them, "Go and look over the land. Pay special attention to Jericho." So, they went out, came to the house of a prostitute named Rahab, and lodged there.

Then the king of Jericho was told, "Look! Israeli men arrived tonight to scout out the land."

So the king of Jericho sent for Rahab and ordered her, "Bring out the men who came to visit you and lodged in your house, because they've come to scout out the entire land."

Now the woman had taken the two men and hid them. So, she replied, "The men really did come to me, but I didn't know from where they came. At dusk, when it was time to close the city gates, the men left. I don't know where the men went. Go after them quickly, and you might overtake them."

But she had taken them up to the roof and had hidden them among stalks of flax that she had laid out in order on the roof. So the men pursued them along the road that leads to the fords of the Jordan River. As soon as the search party had left, they shut the city gate after them. Before the scouts had lain down, she went up to them on the roof "I'm really convinced that the LORD has given you the land," she said, "because we're overwhelmed with fear of you. All the other inhabitants of the land are demoralized at your presence, because we heard how the LORD dried up the water of the Red Sea right in front of you as you were coming out of Egypt, and what you did to the two kings of the Amorites who were on the other side of the Jordan River—to Sihon and Og—whom you completely destroyed. When we heard these reports, we all became terrified and discouraged because of you, for the LORD your God is God in heaven above and on the earth beneath. Now, therefore, since I've treated you so kindly, please swear in the name of the LORD that you'll also be kind to my father's household by giving me this sure sign: Spare my father, my mother, and my brothers and sisters, along with everyone who belongs with them so we won't be killed.

A Promise of Protection

So the men told her, "Our life for yours—even to death—if you don't betray this mission of ours. Then when the Lord gives us this land, we'll treat you graciously and faithfully."

So she let them down by a rope through the window, since her house was built into the town wall where she lived. She told them, "Go out to the hill country, so the search party won't find you, and hide for three days. After that, you may go on your own way."

The men replied, "We'll be free from our commitment to you to which you've obligated us when we invade the land, if you don't tie this rope made with red cords in the window through which you let us down, and if you don't gather your father, your mother, your brothers, and all of the rest of your father's household into your house. Everyone who leaves through the doors of your house into the street will be responsible for his own death, but we'll be responsible for anyone who remains with you in the house if even so much as a hand is laid on him. But if you report this incident, we'll be free from the oath to which you've made us swear."

"Since you put it that way," she replied, "I agree." After she sent them on their way and they had left, she tied the red cord in the window.

The Scouts Report to Joshua

The scouts left for the hill country and remained there for three days until the search party returned. The search party searched the entire road, but was unable to find them. Later, the two men returned from the hill country, crossed over the Jordan River, approached Nun's son Joshua, and told him everything that had happened to them. They reported to Joshua, "The Lord really has given the entire land into our control. The inhabitants of the land have melted away right in front of us!" – Joshua 2:1-24 (ISV)

When Rahab realized that her king intended to harm the spies, she found a perfect hiding place for them.

"But she had brought them up to the roof and hid them with the stalks of flax, which she had laid in order on the roof." – Joshua 2:6 (ISV)

Flax was a plant used for making a soft linen cloth. The coarser parts of the plant were woven together into twine, and the twine eventually braided together into rope. Like many in her day, Rahab probably had a little family business, dyeing cloth and cord up on her roof. But her main business, according to the Bible, was prostitution. These two Israelites had to trust their deliverance to a pagan prostitute.

The Lord often uses humble instruments to do great things. He is using you right now to do something very powerful that will affect the lives of many others. This will affect future generations in your family. Don't quit! Don't give up!

You might wonder how God could bless Rahab—after all, she was a prostitute. However, the Bible is faithful. It records even the failings of God's people.

We all have been in Rahab's shoes at one point in our life—a sinner desperately in need of a Savior. Thank God for sending His only begotten Son to save us all.

The good news is, we don't have to stay in that place of sin and failure. We are now people of faith. Rahab's actions to protect God's people at her own risk came from faith in Him. The Lord looked on her sincere heart. God has mercy on us in our ignorance.

"In the past, God overlooked such ignorance, but now he commands all people everywhere to repent." – Acts 17:30 (NIV)

That goes for all of us as well. Our past is marred by sin, but that's where mercy and grace step in. God had a purpose and a plan for Rahab and used her mightily. It does not matter what's in your past. God isn't holding any of it against you.

He is healing you and delivering you from it right now. He isn't holding anything against you! He doesn't just save us. He redeems us!

The New Testament reveals how Rahab became a faithful follower of the Lord—she is listed as one of the heroes of the faith in Hebrews chapter eleven. She was taken from the dunghill and placed among the saints in the genealogy of the Savior.

Wow.

How awesome is this story? She was related to Jesus. That red cloth she used to signal Joshua represented the blood. She carried the bloodline of Jesus in her veins. Remember this: the devil can't cross the bloodline of Jesus Christ, and this woman was covered in the blood. Her and her family were saved from destruction. They were redeemed, blessed, and honored.

That's what is available to us when we step out in faith —by fasting and praying—to claim the full benefits of the cross.

Prayer

Lord, we plead the blood of Jesus over all of our sins and all of our mistakes, past, present, and future. We come to You and remember all of Your benefits, and we claim them right now in Jesus' name. You forgive all of our sins and heal everything that causes us "dis-ease." We will remember our sins no more, and we will no longer remember the shame of our youth.

We are not cursed, we are blessed. Everything that is meant to harm us will be turned around and used for good, as it says in Romans 8:28. Thank You for healing us of our past, and carrying us forward into a redeemed future—into Your wonderful plan and purpose for our lives. In Jesus' name we pray, amen.

MOMENTS OF WEAKNESS

If you're reading this and you haven't messed up, you're not going to. Stay strong. Keep moving forward. The Lord will give you strength when you are weak, and this time of fasting will be over in just a few days. You're going to make it. Ask Him for strength.

Think about it this way. You're going to see day seven whether you're still fasting or not, so you might as well keep fasting and praying and see your victory!

If you're reading this, and you have messed up, stay focused on God. If you mess up, it's okay. He's not mad at you. Just keep trying till you get it right. Ask the Lord to help you, and He surely will. His grace is sufficient.

There were times in my life that it was such a struggle to fast, and if I messed up, I would just quit. Here's what I found out: Quitters never win. Is it better to make a mistake and keep going, or to just quit altogether? Is there anything in life where we strive for and achieve perfection? And if we don't achieve perfection, we just quit? No! Of course not. We pick ourselves up and keep going!

As I grew closer to the Lord, I realized that messing up was just an opportunity to keep trying and keep going until I got it right. Pray the Lord will strengthen you while you're fasting.

He will give you the power to overcome any temptation. Remember to resist the devil and he will flee in the name of Jesus. In the end, trust me, it is always well worth it every time I fast.

But I'm often under attack. It's like some days everything just goes wrong, but I know it's the enemy trying to mess me up. That's why I just keep marching on. I know victory is mine. And this goes for you too.

Victory is yours.

Don't lose hope but keep the faith. Keep marching on, no matter how hard it is. Do not give up until those walls come down.

It was by faith that the people of Israel marched around Jericho for seven days, and the walls came crashing down. – Hebrews 11:30 (NLT)

Don't give up no matter how hard it is. Hold on. Don't give up.

Even when you feel like you're at your wit's end. When you feel all out of options. Now is not the time to quit.

You have come too far to turn back now. You never know, you might be one more lap away from your victory!

The LORD said to Joshua, "Do not be afraid of them; I have given them into your hand. Not one of them will be able to withstand you." – Joshua 10:8 (NIV)

But thanks be to God! He gives us the victory through our Lord Jesus Christ. – 1 Corinthians 15:57 (NIV)

DAY FIVE
KEEP SILENT

God had a strange plan for the battle of Jericho. He told Joshua to have the armed men march around the city once each day for six days. The priests were to carry the ark, blowing trumpets, but the soldiers were to keep silent.

How hard is it to keep silent when you're going through a battle? You're in an impossible situation, or you're in a valley or trial that never seems to end. Your back is up against that wall. It's hard not to say a word. You might feel like you want to tell every person you come into contact with.

You might want to share your problems on social media. You may want to blame others. Boy, how hard is it to just hold your tongue and keep quiet during these times?

Or maybe you want to set that person straight or tell them what you think they should do. You may want to tell them how you feel, or maybe you just feel like complaining about how horrible things are going for you. The moment we open our mouth up and start speaking this way, we're basically inviting the enemy to set up camp all around us, rob our blessings, and then go in for the kill.

A fool gives full vent to his spirit, but a wise man quietly holds back. – Proverbs 29:11 (ESV)

Set a guard, O LORD, over my mouth; keep watch over the door of my lips! – Psalms 141:3 (ESV)

If you've already given full vent to your spirit, and your mind is racing, all kinds of voices are coming at you, the answer is simple: Just cry out to Jesus Christ right now, and ask Him to rescue you from the attack of the enemy. Then tell Him you're sorry for giving in to it, ask His forgiveness, and enjoy His mercy.

Then turn and go the other way.

God knows what He's doing. He has a plan, a purpose, a reason, a strategy for everything He does.

God told Joshua to tell his army not to say a word. I bet the people inside Jericho were wondering what in the world are they doing? I bet it got the enemy confused.

Exactly!

That's was God's plan—to distract and confuse the enemy.

God's plans are more than we could ever dream up or understand. He's always way ahead of the enemy. But we can come in and mess up God's strategy with our mouths.

Do all things without grumbling or disputing, that you may be blameless and innocent, children of God without blemish in the midst of a crooked and twisted generation, among whom you shine as lights in the world, holding fast to the word of life. – Philippians 2:14-16 (ESV)

We should not let our left hand know what our right hand is doing (Matthew 6:3–4). In other words, what we say to ourselves matters, and sometimes we should not be saying a word.

The Lord works through our silence to fight our battles. God already knows what to do and how to handle the matter. That's why Jesus teaches that when we fast, we should fast in secret (Matthew 6:18).

Just because you are being quiet and not trying to make things happen your own way, don't think God isn't working. Don't think He doesn't see you. He does and will eventually reward you openly, just like He did for Joshua and his army. Through their silence, God was able to speak. When we're fasting and praying it's best to keep our lips zipped around other people.

It's also good to practice being silent before the Lord sometimes.

Do not be quick with your mouth, do not be hasty in your heart to utter anything before God. God is in heaven and you are on earth, so let your words be few. – Ecclesiastes 5:2 (NIV)

Be still, and know that I am God. I will be exalted among the nations, I will be exalted in the earth! – Psalm 46:10 (ESV)

It's hard to hear the voice of God if we're always talking. Sometimes we need to be still and listen to what God is saying. When Joshua and his army were marching around the walls, they were keeping their silence. All that could be heard was the sound of feet marching on the ground.

Wow, how awesome that must have been. I can imagine it right now—all in one mind and one accord —in total obedience to God. The only sound was one of vibrations coming from the ground as the Israelites marched.

Be silent before the Lord, and listen for the sound of His army marching out before you. Can you hear it? They are there—fighting for you as you increase your dependence on God and trust in Him.

Each day you fast, each moment you spend in His presence, you are moving closer to your breakthrough.

You are drawing near to an all-powerful God who has all of the armies of Heaven, and all of the resources in the universe, at His complete disposal.

Prayer

Thank You, Lord, for the gift of silence. Please enable me to be still, be quiet, and hear Your voice. In Jesus' name, amen.

DAY SIX
WALKING AROUND THE WALLS

The Lord told Joshua to walk around the walls for six days in a row, one time each day. For those six times, they were to stay silent as they went. However, on the seventh day they were instructed to walk around seven times, and then blast the horns while the entire army simultaneously gave a loud shout.

Have you ever wondered why the Lord was so specific in His instructions? The number six is the number of mankind (see Revelation 13:18). Man was created on the sixth day. The number seven is significant in the Bible as being a number that represents completeness or perfection. For example, God created a seven-day week that has been in effect ever since the beginning of time.

On the seventh day of marching, the city walls would fall down flat, and then the Israelites were to move in straight away and take the city. The number seven appears eleven times in the second chapter of Joshua. There are seven priests with seven trumpets who march around the city seven days in a row. On the seventh day, they march around seven times.

The Lord is very clearly making a strong point about the number seven!

The number seven in the example of the Jericho story reminds us that God's plan, no matter how foolish or ineffective it may seem to us in the natural, is always perfect and cannot be improved upon by man (see 1 Corinthians 1:18 and Romans 11:33-36; 12:2).

The number seven also makes the very clear point that conquest was part of a spiritual process. Instead of a natural battle, there is a spiritual exercise taking place, and it's designed to display that God's people are set apart unto Him. These are a Holy people that belong to a Holy God. They don't get where they are supposed to go strictly in the natural.

Seven in this story also signifies that the Israelites were in the beginning of a new order. They were coming out of their wilderness time and into their promised land. God is bringing them into something that is good—full of His blessing and protection and provision.

Imagine walking around a major, well-fortified city for those first six days. It certainly took great faith to do this. At any point, they could have been fearful that the enemy would attack them, raining down arrows or other destructive devices from the tops of the walls.

I can imagine that every step they took, they were praying under their breath. With every step they took, their faith got stronger and stronger. The enemy was probably trying to whisper to them and tell them things like:

"You're not going to make it. It's hot. Your mouth is dry. You're making fools out of yourselves. Your legs are tired. Did God really say to do this? This doesn't make any sense. Nothing good is happening. These walls aren't cracking. These people aren't going to just surrender because you're marching around. Who are you kidding?

"Why are you doing this? At any minute, the army of Jericho is going to climb on top of these walls and take you all out. You're sitting ducks!"

But those are all lies. They were completely protected by God to finish their task.

You are protected by God right now. You will not fail this time. The enemy is not going to knock you off of God's path. You're going to finish this task and see the victory. Keep going!

Has the enemy been telling you that the doctor's report is a "fact"? Respond with God's truth! Maybe he's been telling you that financial ruin is your destiny, or that God wants you to suffer and struggle. The Bible says in Psalm 128:2, *"Blessed are all who fear the Lord, who walk in obedience to him. You will eat the fruit of your labor. Blessings and prosperity will be yours."* (NIV)

Are you walking around walls *in obedience to the Lord* right now? Then blessings and prosperity are yours!

Are you in an oppressive work situation? Is your boss impossible to work with? Start earnestly praying for God to save, bless, protect, heal, and prosper that person, and then watch God move!

Is your marriage in trouble? Speak and pray and claim God's truth over your marriage:

Therefore what God has joined together, let no one separate. – Mark 10:9 (NIV)

Let marriage be held in honor among all. – Hebrews 13:4 (ESV)

In the same way husbands should love their wives as their own bodies. He who loves his wife loves himself. – Ephesians 5:28 (ESV)

However, let each one of you love his wife as himself, and let the wife see that she respects her husband. – Ephesians 5:33 (ESV)

If your husband has made bad decisions or hasn't treated you well, pray for that man. Pray that God will put forgiveness in your heart. Pray that He will protect and bless your husband and turn him away from sin.

For the man who does not love his wife but divorces her, says the Lord, the God of Israel, covers his garment with violence, says the Lord of hosts. So guard yourselves in your spirit, and do not be faithless. – Malachi 2:16 (ESV)

Your husband may need you to intercede for him right now more than anyone realizes.

Whatever your specific situation is, just realize that what is impossible with man is possible with God. He can heal, repair, and restore even the most broken of situations.

Just look at what Joshua and his army were dealing with. Massive walls were standing in their way, and God's answer wasn't to get a battering ram. God's answer was a spiritual exercise—an exercise of faith—to march around the walls and let Him bring them down.

They didn't look at the problem. They looked to God. They didn't let the wall stand in their way. Yes, it was big, but they knew their God was bigger.

We serve a big God who *cannot* fail.

I remember as a child, one time my mother needed a car. So my mother, my father, and I all walked around a car 7 times. That seems crazy, but guess what? It worked. Just a short time later, my mother had a car.

That was not the only time my mother did that. I can look back and remember her doing that many times—

literally marching around God's promised blessings. It was a way she was exercising her faith.

Actions speak louder than words.

Fasting and praying seem passive to us, but they are actually bold actions—exercises in faith and obedience to an all-powerful God. Just like Joshua and the Israelites were activating and exercising their faith by walking around the walls, you are walking around your walls right now.

And God is moving. He's working. He's acting on your behalf right now, even though you can't see it just yet. Keep believing. Keep trusting. And keep marching. Don't you even think about giving up now.

These walls are coming down!

Prayer

Lord, thank You for all that You have done and for bringing me this far. Let my faith continue to rise. Help me to never cease trusting and believing in You.

Lord, I know that You can take the impossible and make it possible. I declare today that I will choose faith over fear. With Your help, through the power of the Holy Spirit, I will stand firm on Your promises.

I know You have plans for me—plans to prosper me and not to harm me. Plans to give me hope and a future.

So I'm going to believe it and declare it, and get ready to receive it, in the mighty name of Jesus, amen!

Moreover, brethren, I declare to you the gospel which I preached to you, which also you received and in which you stand. – 1 Corinthians 15:1 (NKJV)

DAY SEVEN

VICTORY

Well, here you are. This is it. The last day of your fast. Just like the Israelites made it through their challenge of faith and finally reached that 7th day, you've made it.

Remember that 7 represents completion. On this day, it is finished.

The Lord has raised the banner of victory.

The time has come.

The Israelites had been through so much, and they probably felt like this day would never come. They probably felt like it took forever, knowing that at the end, this wall would come down. By faith, they looked forward to victory.

By faith, they received their promise.

You're about to receive what you've waited for your whole life.

How good does it feel to know that your victory is here?

It's an indescribable feeling.

When the Israelites marched out on the seventh day, the wall was still standing. But by faith, they received their victory on that seventh day.

Can you see it today—by faith?

Can you open your spiritual eyes and see your victory today?

I can only imagine how Joshua and the Israelites must have felt. They had made it.

But there was one last thing.

The priests had to blow the trumpets, and the people had to shout. They had held their shouts in until given the word. They had to wait for God. The ark of the Lord—representative of His presence—was out in front. His people were behind, ready to shout.

Boy did that ever confuse and scare the enemy.

Imagine them changing pace, blowing the trumpets and horns, and giving that shout!

They were rolling out a red carpet for the King of Kings because His manifest presence was showing up on the scene to give victory!

They were blowing the trumpet to declare victory before the battle even started!

Victory Is Yours

The Israelites finally got to see their victory. They refused to stop till it was finished. They held onto their promises from the Lord. They for sure weren't going to let a wall stand in between them and their promised land.

Don't let a wall stand between you and your promised land. Look what God has done for you. Didn't He bring you out of Egypt, from the bondage of sin? Didn't He part the Red Sea in your life? Didn't He give you manna when you were hungry? Didn't He give you living water to drink when you were thirsty?

Didn't He dry the ground for you to cross over your Jordan and bring you to your promised land? You have made it, and it's time to declare what God has done for you. Declare it time and time again. Take a minute and thank Him, for He is worthy to be praised.

The Lord left us the best instruction manual ever and that's the Bible. When we put it into action, as we have already been doing, we will surely see walls come down. The Lord is creating open spaces for you. He wants the best for you, and the enemy knows that.

Blowing the Trumpet

Blowing a trumpet wasn't a practice that was only associated with battles and wars. Trumpets were also blown during times of celebration, like when people gathered for a feast. In Isaiah, the trumpet sound was used to assemble people to fast and pray. In Joel 2, it is used as a warning, "Blow the trumpet in Zion, sound an alarm on my holy mountain!" (ESV)

In the book of Psalms, we find the trumpet sounded to praise and worship God. In all of these cases, when the trumpet was blown, it shifted the atmosphere.

You probably don't have an actual trumpet on hand, and that's okay. God blows His breath through us, and we actually become God's trumpet. His instrument!

We have to breathe in the very breath of God. The Holy Spirit is often likened to "wind" or "breath." In fact, the original Greek word that gets translated as "Spirit" is *pneuma*, and it literally means "wind" or "breath."

Before the Israelites could let out a shout, they needed the breath of God in them. They needed Holy Spirit power!

Take a deep breath right now, and say "Breathe on me, oh breath of God." Ask God the Father for more of the Holy Spirit. Ask Him to come in and fill you, and immerse you in His Spirit. He always gives more of the Holy Spirit to those who ask!

"If you then, though you are evil, know how to give good gifts to your children, how much more will your Father in heaven give the Holy Spirit to those who ask him!" – Luke 11:13 (NIV)

The Israelites had the breath of God blowing through them to shake the foundations and break open the city gates. The earth quaked. The walls crumbled.

Their voices were like dynamite because God's voice was literally coming through them. They had *dunamis* power—Holy Spirit power—flowing through them at that moment.

I believe that's why the Israelites had to stay silent up to that point. God wanted them to know that their own voices—their own power, their own strength, their own efforts—had nothing to do with it. It was His voice, His Word, His power that brought down the walls.

This was a completely supernatural event that took place.

Let the voice of God flow through you right now.

Be His trumpet, and let Him blow His power and presence right through you. Yield yourself completely to Him, and be His instrument.

Speak His words.

The victory is in your shout!

The enemy can't rob your praise.

Your shout is a weapon!

It's tearing down walls right now!

Keep Shouting

If you can, find something to walk around that is symbolic of your problem. For example, if you're dealing with sickness, throw the doctor's papers in the floor and walk around those. It could be something that represents a marital problem, a financial problem —whatever you're dealing with.

Now, start slowly walking around that problem. You're going to do it seven times.

As you walk, know that you are not walking alone. Others are reading this book too. Let's unify. Let's believe for each other as we do this.

As you walk around, raise your voice. The time has come. Ask God to breathe through you right now. Be His mouthpiece. Let Him speak through you.

Prophesy.

Speak to those walls and command them to fall in Jesus' name!

Strongholds are coming down, right now in Jesus' name!

Marriages are being healed, in Jesus' name!

Sickness and disease are fleeing right now, in Jesus' name!

Bodies are being healed!

Dead things are being raised!

Finances are being restored!

Relationships are being repaired!

Shame has to go, because I am forgiven. I will no longer remember the shame of my youth!

Rejection cannot stay here, because I am accepted in the beloved by Jesus Christ!

I am not an orphan. I have been adopted into the family of God!

Fear and doubt leave now because I'm a child of God, and I have been given power, love, and a sound mind! I have the mind of Christ!

Bitterness, unforgiveness, rage, anger, and malice all have to flee!

Discord and disharmony have to go, because we are loosing unity, harmony, and peace!

We are loosing forgiveness, gentleness, understanding, kindness, goodness, and love in Jesus' name!

Say it loud: The devil has to flee my marriage, my family, my children, my body, my health, my finances, my business, my job, my environment, my reputation, and my life because Jesus Christ is on the throne! He reigns in all of those places! He reigns in every area of my heart, mind, and life and there is victory, healing, and blessing in every area of my life in Jesus' name!

Now give God a big shout of praise!

KEEP WALKING IN VICTORY

I *have given you authority to trample on snakes and scorpions and to overcome all the power of the enemy; nothing will harm you.* – Luke 10:19 (NIV)

You just received your victory. There is no doubt about that.

Stay in faith. Know that God has heard and shifted everything in regard to this situation, and has given you the victory.

Yes, it is manifesting even now. The spiritual realm has been moved through your obedience—through your prayers. Your fasting. Your faith.

Maintain your faith, knowing that God has heard and answered, and the enemy has to flee. He doesn't like leaving, but he has to. He cannot stay where a child of God has exercised their God-given authority.

When we stand in the authority Jesus gave us, the demons have to flee. But as they flee, they tend to try to convince you that they aren't leaving.

All the while, they are literally having to move further and further away from you until there is no longer any trace of them. It's nothing more than a last, desperate attempt to throw a few more lies at you as they go. They're trying to see if they can get you to believe any of them, but you're not going to!

Don't believe them.

You just had an amazing victory, and everything in your life is going to start getting better from this moment forward. The spiritual realm was shifted today, and your life will never be the same. That is certain.

Stay in good spirits, and keep your faith active and strong. Choose the joy of the Lord. He wants you to have joy and gladness. He wants to give you beauty for ashes. Believe Him for that today. His Word says that's what He wants for you, and He does not lie.

"To all who mourn in Israel, he will give a crown of beauty for ashes, a joyous blessing instead of mourning, festive praise instead of despair. In their righteousness, they will be like great oaks that the LORD has planted for his own glory." – Isaiah 61:3 (NLT)

There was a time when I was walking around spiritually deflated. I didn't want to sing anymore. My praise was gone. One day I heard the Lord say, "Sing, My daughter."

I began to pray that spirit of defeat and fear off of me, and I felt the Lord blow through me. A Lauren Daigle song came to my mind, and I began to sing, "Breathe, oh breath of God..."

It was a breath of fresh air.

It blew through me, and my worship was back.

My shout was back louder and stronger than ever before. I was renewed and revived. We have to continually cultivate an attitude of faith and victory in our lives.

A lot of times, after big spiritual victories, we get back into the routines of life. Over time, if we're not careful, we'll fall into new traps the enemy sets. We can end up walking around spiritually deflated and not even know it.

Think about an inner tube. If it's only halfway blown up, it's not floating too well. It isn't much good to anyone. It needs some air back in it to be useful.

God wants to keep the walls down. Now that our walls are down, He also wants to use us to help others get their walls down. But He can't do that if we walk around spiritually deflated. We need to always be going back to our source—back to the Father, asking Him to fill us with Holy Spirit power.

Fasting Is a New Weapon in Your Arsenal

The closer and deeper you are in your walk with the Lord, the more fasting becomes a lifestyle. You can be more spiritually connected to the Lord when you fast, so whenever you are faced with a difficult situation, always remember this powerful weapon that you have on hand. Fasting is a necessity for certain times and certain types of spiritual warfare (see Matthew 17:21).

Fasting keeps you humble and strengthens your spirit. Fasting builds up your faith. Fasting knocks walls down.

Fasting moves mountains. Fasting breaks every chain. Fasting renews your mind.

Fasting takes your prayer life to the next level. Fasting takes you from glory to glory.

For the rest of your days, always remember this wonderful tool, and use it whenever you need it!

MEET CALLED WRITERS

Please visit **CalledWriters.com** for articles, videos, and other resources by anointed, Spirit-led authors and ministers!

We are a relatively new Christian publishing house, dedicated to bringing you authors who are divinely gifted, anointed, and called by God for such a time as this.

We would love to connect with you on social media as well:

Facebook.com/CalledWriters

Twitter: @CalledWriters

Instagram: @CalledWriters

RECENT RELEASES FROM CALLED WRITERS

*Speaking in Tongues: Enjoying Intimacy With God
Through Tongues and Interpretation*

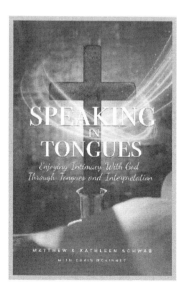

Available on Amazon

Available on Amazon

ABOUT THE AUTHOR

Rhoda is a wife, mother, and minister. Her life is a wonderful picture of godly restoration. She is also an intercessory prayer warrior who operates in the gifts of prophecy and healing.

Rhoda loves speaking and ministering to people in church services, healing services, and prayer services.

For bookings, please fill out the contact form at: RhodaFayeDiehl.com

Rhoda also ministers to people online in the following places:

Facebook.com/rhodafaye.diehl

Twitter.com/RhodaDiehl

Instagram.com/rhodafayediehl

Any readers who would like to share a testimony of how God used this book to work in your life, please feel free to email: rhodafaye1980@yahoo.com

Printed in Great Britain
by Amazon